KUN YOGA

ALL ABOUT OUR CHAKRA!

BESTSELLING AUTHOR

Shreyananda Natha

Cover & Graphic Design

Mattias Långström

Contact: oneofakindbooks@bhagwan.se

Kundalini Yoga

ALL ABOUT OUR CHAKRA!

BESTSELLING AUTHOR

Shreyananda Natha

Copyright © Mattias Långström

ISBN: 9798476988687

✻✻✻

Publisher: BHAGWAN 2021

No part of this publication may be reproduced or transmitted in any form, or by any means, electronic or mechanical, including photocopying, scanning, recording, or any information storage and retrieval sýstem, without express written permission from the publisher, except for the inclusion of brief quotations embodied in critical articles and reviews. This book is a work of fiction and a product of the author´s imagination.

Namasté

I want to thank the teachers and students I have had over the years and who have made my journey with yoga so interesting. Thank you for all the inspiration you have given me and for making this book possible. The yoga masters who no longer live among us, live on with every new person who immerses themselves in the yoga tradition.

Sri Swami Sivananda, Sri Swami Satyananda, Sri Tirumalai Krishnamacharya, Sri Swami Vishnudevananda, Sri K. Pattabhi Jois, Osho, Swami Nirdosha, Swami Omananda, Swami Janakananda, Ole Schmidt, Turiya, Maryam Abrishami and Sanna Kuittinen.

Everyone who has searched for answers to what they perceived through an activated ajna chakra. In yoga, they have learned the principles behind the universe, the collective consciousness, and the creative power, Kundalini Shakti. The duality behind everything, both what we see and what we do not see. Together we help to pass on the previous secret knowledge, about our gunas, nadis, and chakras, to anyone who wants to be seen.

THE AUTHOR

Shreyananda Natha is the author of over twelve titles on yoga. Among other things, he has written the most comprehensive books on yoga in Swedish – Everything About Yoga and the study book The Yoga Bible. He is also a certified yoga and meditation teacher according to EYTF's international guidelines and has undergone a multi-year yoga teacher training under the leadership of Swami Omananda at Satyananda Ashram. Shreyananda Natha holds the highest initiation in the Tantric Natha Order. He travels frequently to Asia and India to improve himself, and to gain knowledge and inspiration. He has immersed himself in the tantric rituals and is known for his extensive knowledge of yoga, deep relaxation, and meditation

There is no authority that can say what yoga is. When you give yourself fully and completely, and experience yoga without limitations or doubts, when you become one with the true experience in yourself, the real encounter with yoga arises. Only then do you understand what yoga is – for you. You are no longer limited by ornament, shyness and artificial thought patterns that lie as a filter between you and the transformation. Yoga is a cultural-historical wealth that is still passed on from teacher to student and helps man to find his way back to his true nature. It opens us up and attracts awareness. It strengthens our self-esteem, and our entire person's spectrum of possibilities suddenly becomes visible to us. Yoga is not difficult. You do not have to be vegan or able to stand on your head. You just need to practice your yoga regularly and the rest will come by itself.

With all the love from the universe – Aum Shanti Shreyananda Natha.

KUNDALINI YOGA

WHAT IS KUNDALINI?

Kundalini is what we call the dormant energy that exists in every human being. It has its seat at the bottom of the spine in the perineum, or pelvic floor, (between the urine and the excretory organs) in men and at the cervix (the bottom of the cervix in women). This is also where the Mooladhara chakra is found.

With the help of yogic techniques such as asana, pranayama, Kriya yoga and meditation, one can increase the flow of prana in the body and direct it down to Mooladhara in order to awaken the Kundalini shakti. When the Kundalini energy then begins to rise upwards along the Sushumna nadi and through the chakras, the dormant parts of the brain that are in contact with the respective chakras are awakened. Through this process, we can have greater access to the capacity of our brain and raise our consciousness.

Awakening of Kundalini should be done slowly and systematically. The body and mind should be prepared slowly. This way, you avoid any risks that a rise may entail. One should not try to control or influence the mind as such. The mind is an "extension" of the body and therefore it is easiest to start with the body and gradually move on with prana, nadis and chakras.

HOW THE KUNDALINI WAS DISCOVERED
Since the beginning, man has been involved in, and experienced events of a supernatural nature. When it so happened that one would feel what others were thinking and wanting, the inner visions manifested and dreams came true. It was noticed that a certain crowd of people had a very special ability to express their creativity through art, music and poetry. Some people had a strong drive, zest for life while others barely managed to get up in the morning. Man became curious as to what was the cause of these differences. In the end, through one's own experience, one could come to the conclusion that in man there was a special form of energy. In some, this energy was dormant, in development in others, and fully awakened in very few. This energy was called after gods and deities. After they also discovered prana, they started calling it prana shakti. In Tantrism, this energy is called Kundalini shakti.

DIFFERENT NAMES

In Sanskrit, Kundalini means "spiral" or "something that is rolled up". Kundalini shakti has thus traditionally been described as something that has just been rolled up. Nevertheless, the meaning of the whole thing has often been misunderstood. Kundalini actually derives from the word - kunda, which refers to "a deeper place", or a pit. The place where a dead body is burned is also called a customer. The word Kundalini refers to Shakti, or the power, energy in its dormant state. When it then wakes up and manifests itself, it is called Devi, Kali, Durga, Saraswati, Lakshmi or something else depending on the characteristics and qualities that it evokes in man.

In Christianity, terms such as "the path of the initiated" or "the stairs to heaven" are used. These refer to the Kundalini that rise along the sushumna. The Christian cross symbolizes Kundalini rising and the resulting spiritual beauty. In all spiritual paths, whether one is talking about samadhi, nirvana, moksha, unity, kaivalya or liberation, it is Kundalini awakening one is referring to.

KUNDALINI, DURGA, KALI

When you can handle a raised Kundalini in a positive way, its quality is called Durga. If Kundalini instead wakes up when you are still unprepared and not ready to handle it, it is called Kali.

The goddess Kali is illustrated as naked, black in color and she wears a rosary of one hundred and eight human skulls that represent memories from previous lives. Her blood-red outstretched tongue symbolizes rajo guna whose circular movement pattern gives power to all creative activity. She wants to urge sadhakas to take control of rajo guna.

Durga is a beautiful goddess who is illustrated riding a tiger. She has eight arms that represent the eightfold elements. She wears a rosary with fifty-two human skulls that symbolize her wisdom, power and the fifty-two letters of the Sanskrit alphabet. Durga eliminates all the evil consequences that life can carry with it, and comes with power and peace. This force is released from Mooladhara.

KUNDALINI PHYSIOLOGY

When Kundalini begins to rise, it passes different phases on its way up to the cosmic consciousness - Shiva, where they finally merge. The highest consciousness - Shiva, has its seat in Sahasrara - the super consciousness, at the top of the head. In the Vedic texts as well as in Tantrism, this seat is called Hiranyagarbha - the womb of consciousness. It is connected to the pituitary gland. Just below there is another psychic center called the Ajna chakra which is connected to the pineal gland, the seat of intuitive consciousness. It is located at the top of the spine and at the height of the eyebrow center - bhrumadhya. Ajna chakra is important as it is connected to both Mooladhara and Sahasrara chakra.

Chakras are energy vortices that are experienced to vibrate and rotate at different speeds. There are thousands of chakras in the human body. In tantra and yoga, only a few are used for filling the entire spectrum of human evolution and life - physically and mentally, from the rough to the polished. There are six chakras that have a direct connection to the dormant parts of the brain.

Through nadis, energy flows to and from the chakras. Nadis are channels where prana (vital) and mana (mental) energy flows through and out to all parts of the body. There are about seventy-two thousand nadis. Three of these are extra important as they control the flow of prana and the consciousness of all other nadis. These are ida, pingala and sushumna. Ida controls all the mental activity and pingala all the vital activity. Ida is known as the moon and pingala as the sun. Sushumna is the channel for the flow of spiritual consciousness. Ida and pingala do not flow in the body at the same time but they alternate. When the left nostril is open, ida nadi flows and when the right nostril is open, the pingala flows. When the pingala flows, the left part of the brain is active and when the ida flows, the right part of the brain is active. In this way, nadis control our brain, way of acting and consciousness.

If you can get prana and chitta, ie. ida and pingala flow at the same time, you can also get both halves of the brain to cooperate in thinking and action. This does not happen in our normal daily lives. For this to happen, it is required that the sushi humna is in contact with Kundalini shakti.

Sushumna nadi is like a hollow tube with three more tubes in it. One is more subtle than the other. These tubes, or nadis, are called sushumna (denotes tamas), vajrini (denotes rajas), chitrini (denotes sattva) and Brahma (denotes consciousness). The highest consciousness born of Kundalini shakti passes through Brahma.

When Kundalini wakes up, the sushumna passes up to the Ajna chakra. Mooladhara acts as a powerful engine. To start this engine, pranic energy is needed and it is created with the help of pranayamas. The prana is then directed downwards in the body, to the Mooladhara chakra. From there it is then directed upwards towards the Ajna chakra. If the sushumna nadi is not open, the energy cannot be distributed, which means that the prana remains in the Mooladhara chakra.

Ida and pingala nadi are constantly flowing but their power is weak. It is only when the sushumna is awakened that enlightenment can take place. Kundalini yoga is based on awakening the sushumna, and when awakened, the contact between the highest and lowest levels of consciousness is enabled. Then Kundalini can wake up and rise from Mooladhara up along the sushumna and then become one with Shiva in Sahasrara.

THE MYSTICAL TREE
In Bhagavad Gita you can read about the immortal tree that grows up and down, with the roots up and the leaves and branches down. It is said that he who knows the tree also knows the truth of life. This tree is found in the human body and nervous system. Thoughts, feelings, obstacles, etc. symbolized by the leaves of the tree. The brain is symbolized by the roots and the spine of the trunk. You have to climb from the top of the tree (in this case from the root) and up to the roots. In Kabbalah, this tree is called the "tree of life". In the Bible it is called the "tree of knowledge." Anyone who tries to move upwards from Mooladhara to Sahasrara thus climbs to the roots.

KUNDALINI AND OUR BRAIN
Humans are often said to use only a tenth of the full capacity of the brain. The knowledge we have, what we think and do is stored in this small part. The rest is known as the dormant and inactive part of the brain. The reason it

is inactive is that the amount of energy is not enough to keep it awake. The active part of the brain gets its energy from ida and pingala nadi while the dormant part only has access to pingala ie. prana, or, life energy. It lacks conscious energy, ie. ida, or, manas.

To awaken the sleeping part of the brain, we must charge the front part of the brain with prana and consciousness. We must also awaken sushumna nadi. We do this by practicing pranayamas regularly for an extended period of time. With the help of Kundalini yoga, one could discover that the different parts of the brain were connected to our chakras. To access dormant parts of the brain, one must work on awakening the chakras in the body. Chakras can be described as switches.

The same way, the Mooladhara chakra is used as a "switch" to awaken Kundalini, which actually has its seat in Sahasrara, but most of us find it easier to get in touch with Mooladhara. Each chakra works individually. This means that if Kundalini wakes up in Mooladhara, it goes straight from there up to Sahasrara. Or, if it wakes up in Swadhisthana, it also goes from there straight up to Sahasrara. Kundalini can be awakened in a chakra or collectively in all chakras at the same time. When Kundalini awakens in an individual chakra, the consciousness is filled with what is characteristic of that particular chakra.

WHAT KUNDALINI SHAKTI REALLY IS

There are many different descriptions of what Kundalini shakti really is. Many yogis believe that Kundalini shakti is pranic energy that flows through the sushumna associated with the spine. They believe that Kundalini is part of the pranic flow in our energy body and that there is no physical / anatomical equivalent.

Other yogis experience Kundalini as part of the signals that flow along the nerve pathways and that travel along the spinal cord up to specific parts of the brain. However, most agree that the experience of Kundalini is something psychophysiological that is manifested in the spine.

METHODS FOR AWAKENING:

In Tantrism, various techniques are used to awaken Kundalini shakti. These can be practiced individually or in combination with each other.

AWAKENED IN CONNECTION WITH BIRTH
A few children are born with an already awake Kundalini. These children look at life very clearly, have a highly developed way of thinking and a very unusual way of looking at life. They often have no normal social relationship with their parents because they see them as "those who gave them life".

MANTRA
It is a powerful, gentle and risk-free method. However, it requires patience, time, discipline and regularity. Through mantra repetition and the vibration of sound, a wave of patterns is created that affects the mind. The physical, mental and emotional body is cleansed. It is important to focus the mantra on something by, for example, focusing on the tip of the nose or a chakra.

TAPASYA
It is a psychological procedure where you start a process that from the root eliminates bad habits that have created weakness and hinder develop-

ment and willpower. Willpower is the core of tapasya. To enable the development and willpower, you want to curb the inner fire, live in celibacy, say no to lust, be restrained and, deny your own desires.

ASUHADHI - Using Herbs
This is the fastest and most effective method besides tantric initiation. It should not be confused with the use of drugs. Asuhadhi is a risky method that should only be done under the guidance of a guru.

RAJA YOGA
With Raja yoga, one merges the individual consciousness with the universal superconscious. This is done step by step with the help of concentration, meditation and the experience of unity with the absolute and highest self. When you focus and calm the mind, the sushum opens, which enables the rising of Kundalini. This is a mild method that is experienced to be difficult by many because it requires a lot of patience and discipline.

PRANAYAMA
Pranayamas are very powerful. If you are well

prepared, live healthy, have a calm and safe place to practice breathing exercises, Kundalini can be awakened very quickly. Pranayamas strongly affect the body, creating heat while lowering the temperature in the inner body. Breathing changes the pattern of brain waves. It is important to cleanse the body with the help of shatkarmas before entering the process in order to better handle the rapid changes that come. Breathing is the link between Hatha and Kundalini yoga.

KRIYA YOGA
This is the simplest method for people living in the modern world. Here you do not have to confront the mind as in e.g. Raja yoga. People who are Sattvic may find it easy to awaken Kundalini through Raja yoga, but if you have a tumultuous mind that is constantly in motion, it only creates even more tension, guilt, complexes and sometimes even schizophrenia. When practicing Kriya yoga, Kundalini shakti is awakened slowly and methodically.

TANTRIC INITIATION
This method requires an understanding of what Shiva and Shakti stand for. You have to change your approach to passions and desires in life.

Under the guidance of a guru, this is the fastest way to Kundalini awakening.

SHAKTIPAT
This method is performed by a guru. One experiences a temporary state of awakening - samadhi.

SURRENDER YOURSELF
This path means that one does not strive to awaken Kundalini Shakti. You let it happen when it happens and if it happens. It is believed that a strong enough will can arouse Kundalini.

PREPARATIONS
It is important to learn Kundalini yoga from a competent teacher so that one knows for sure that the process is going the right way. It is also important to be physically, mentally and emotionally prepared. Waking up Kundalini shakti can take time and you can count on it being a long process. However, there is nothing that says that Kundalini cannot wake up quickly. What really takes time is learning to keep the Kundalini alive.

It is important that the sushumna is open, otherwise Kundalini will rise along the ida or pingala which leads to complications. The elements, chakras and nadis must also be purified in order for Kundalini to flow freely. This is done with the help of asanas, pranayamas and Hatha yoga shatkarmas.

Surya namaskar and surya bheda pranayama cleanses pingala nadi. Shatkarmas and pranayamas open up the sushumna. You start by cleaning the elements with shat karma. Then continue with asanas and pranayamas. After that you can continue with mudras and bandhas. Then you are ready to start with Kriya yoga.

KARMA YOGA
Karma yoga is a very important part of spiritual development. Without Karma yoga, evolution will stop no matter what method one chooses to follow. Karma yoga prepares the mind. Positive and negative partners become visible, consciousness is broadened and concentration is strengthened. Karma yoga is not a direct cause of Kundalini awakening but an important part of the process.

DIFFERENT AWAKENINGS
It is important to be able to distinguish between

the awakening of Kundalini, chakras and sushumna nadi. It should also be possible to distinguish between an awakening between Mooladhara and Kundalini. The first step in awakening Kundalini shakti is to create harmony between ida and pingala nadi. The next step is to awaken the chakra system which leads to the sushumna opening and which allows for the Kundalini shakti to wake up.

When the process takes place in this order, you do not have to worry about negative consequences. If Kundalini instead wakes up before the sushumna is open, the energy will remain in the Mooladhara chakra and create sexual and neurotic disorders. Should any chakra not be open, Kundalini will get stuck in its path and create stagnation in development.

Harmony between ida and pingala nadi.

Pingala stands for the vital energy in the body. Ida stands for conscious energy. These two nadis control the two hemispheres of the brain, which in turn control all activity in the body. It is not really the awakening of these two that one strives for but a synchronization between them. As is well known, these control the body's temperature, digestion, hormonal secretion, the brain waves and the whole body's system. Bad food and lifestyle disturbs and creates an imbalance between them, which leads to physical and mental illness. Sushumna can only wake up when ida and pingala flow in harmony. Hatha yoga, pranayamas and Raja yoga are the best methods to create harmony between ida and pingala. Especially nadi shodhana.

Awaken the chakras.

All chakras must be balanced before the sushumna can wake up. Every little part of the body is connected to a chakra. Asanas open up the chakras in a gentle way. Sometimes a chakra can open quickly. Then feelings of fear, anxiety, passion, depression, etc. can emerge that have connections to previous experiences from previous lives.

Awaken the Sushumna.

It takes a lot of patience to awaken the sushumna nadi. You can expect to have experiences of a more intense nature than those that come when a chakra is awakened. These experiences are often completely illogical and strange. Hatha yoga and pranayamas are essential for awakening sushumna nadi.

KUNDALINI SINKS IN
After a rise, Kundalini will fall again. But the mind and consciousness will still be affected and changed. You get a higher state of consciousness. Our whole lives and our thoughts are affected. Emotions, body, and mind. Kundalini will be what characterizes life.

When Shiva and Shakti become one in Sahasrara, one experiences samadhi and silent parts of the brain wake up. In this state, one is completely unaware of opposites, man and woman, Shiva and Shakti - everything is one and the same. During the experience of samadhi, Bindu develops. Bindu means point and encompasses the entire cosmos. It is the seat of human intelligence and of all creation. After a while, the Bindu is divided into two and the duality of Shiva and Shakti becomes reality again.

Samadhi can be likened to the condition of an infant. One does not know the difference between man and woman and there is no physical or sexual difference. When Shiva and Shakti return to the rough plane, down to the Mooladhara chakra, they separate. Duality exists in the mind in the world that consists of name and form but not in samadhi.

When Kundalini sinks and you return to physical reality, you do it with a changed consciousness. You may live your life just as before, with the same patterns, desires and passions. What makes the difference is that you observe life as if it were a spectacle.

You are in the theater of life just as before but as a spectator. The changed consciousness is manifested through one. You are in contact with the parts of the brain that were previously silent. One is in contact with the knowledge, power and wisdom of the universe.

THE EXPERIENCE OF THE AWAKENING
A Kundalini rise can be likened to an explosion that takes you from one plane of consciousness to another plane of being. You travel through the borderland where perceptions, feelings and experiences change character. It is a journey between what you have experienced and the inexperienced.

The awakening takes place step by step and can take time. The preliminary awakening, and usually the first step, is the experience of light at bhrumadhya. This usually develops over a long period of time, in a very mild way and rarely creates any negative experiences. After a while, your appetite and need for sleep may decrease and your mind is still.

When the Kundalini rise finally takes place, it happens with power and sometimes you can experience things that are difficult to comprehend. One of the most common experiences is the feeling of "a current" along the spine. One can experience a burning sensation in Mooladhara and an energy flowing up and down along the sushumna. You can also hear sounds in the form of drums, bells, music, birds and flutes. You can also experience anger, passion and other repressed emotions that emerge. This usually passes within a few days. Some develop Siddhis which after a while also disappear.

You can lose your appetite for weeks, become depressed, lose interest in life and experience everything as very sad at the same time as the mind can become very mobile and creative. You might start writing poetry, creating music or some other art. This flattens out after a while and you land in your normal life and normal everyday life again. From the outside, everything looks like before, but you have an increased inner awareness and ability to observe. Headaches and insomnia can occur in some people when Kundalini wakes up.

It is easy to confuse the awakening of our chakras, nadis and sushumna with a Kundalini rise. When the chakra is opened, you get experiences that are usually pleasant and satisfying. They are rarely nasty or scary. When you get pleasant experiences during meditation or the kirtan or can feel the presence of your guru, it is a chakra awakening that takes place and not Kundalini.

When sushumna wakes up, you can experience the spine as shining or as a streak of light. You can also have sensual experiences that can seem very confusing and illogical. You can smell, hear screams or cry, feel warm or experience pain. Sometimes you can get disease symptoms and fever that doctors can not diagnose. When sushumna wakes up, you go through a form of depression, anorexia and loneliness. You begin to understand your inner being, your true nature. Materia is experienced as nothing and the body feels as if it were made of air or you can feel as if you are not a part of the body. You can communicate with your surroundings, trees, animals and water. You can start to anticipate things, but usually only boredom, accidents and disasters. You can feel reluctant to do work and it is good if at this stage you can be close to your guru to explain what is happening.

Fine visions and experiences are not always a sushumna or Kundalini awakening. It can still be chakras that open up, or experiences of samskaras and archetypes that emerge as a result of the sadhana that one follows. But to roughly sum it up, one can say that a Kundalini awakening always creates more abilities, Siddhis. If you slowly begin to understand language better, all of a sudden start to understand complicated things, all of a sudden become good at cooking, all of a sudden get a hearing in music, etc., then a gradual Kundalini awakening is taking place. If you experience temporary sensations and powerful light phenomena or visions, there may be other things that are connected to your chakras.

DIET

When Kundalini is awakened, it is extremely important to follow a proper diet as the food affects the mind and human nature. During awakening, physical changes occur in the body, mainly in the digestive system. The body's internal temperature drops drastically and is much lower compared to the outer body temperature. Metabolism is slow and oxygen consumption decreases. The food must therefore be easy to break down.

The best is cooked food. Crushed wheat, barley, lentils and dal are preferred. Preferably in liquid form. Fatty and heavy foods should be avoided and the amount of protein should be kept to a minimum, as they strain the liver and require a lot of energy to be able to be broken down. When the mind undergoes a change, the liver works hard.

It is good to increase the carbohydrates in the diet such as rice, potatoes, wheat, and corn. These cause the internal body temperature to increase and do not require much energy to digest.

Spices play a very important role for a Kundalini

yogi. Coriander, cumin, anise, black pepper, green pepper, cayenne, mustard seeds, cardamom, cinnamon, etc. support digestion. They store vital energy and support the internal body temperature.

KRIYA YOGA
Awakening Kundalini is difficult. Most yogic and religious paths are based on a lot of rules that require incredible self-discipline. Rishis in the tantric tradition developed a series of exercises that would be easy to follow and apply, regardless of lifestyle, beliefs or desires. Kriya yoga is seen as one of the most powerful of all tantric exercises and the path that is most suitable for modern man. The purpose of Kriya yoga is to open up the chakra system, purify the nadis and finally awaken the Kundalini shakti. Through the various kriyas, Kundalini is aroused gradually. It does not rise suddenly, which would be too difficult to handle.

Unlike other religions and yogic paths that often require strong mind control, in Kriya yoga one should not worry about the mind. Even if you can not concentrate or calm your mind, it does not matter - you develop anyway. Rishis in Kriya yoga believe that control of the mind is not necessary.

"Keep practicing and let the mind do what it does. In time, consciousness will reach the point where the mind no longer disturbs."

It is not always the fault of the mind that it is anxious or restless. Hormones, indigestion and a weak energy flow in the nervous system can be the cause. One should never blame the mind when it is restless, not even oneself. You are not stupid, bad, unclean or horrible even if you think evil thoughts. Everyone suffers from these, even the most peaceful and devoted. Trying to push back from the mind and thoughts and then see them come back again creates a division and in worst case causes mental illness. There is no good or evil mind. They are both one and the same. The mind is nothing but energy. Anger, passion, gratitude and joy are all different forms of the same energy. In Kriya yoga, one tries to utilize this energy without trying to silence or dampen it in any way.

In Kriya yoga, one does not try to concentrate or meditate. Mental control is not the purpose. The mind should flow freely and naturally. Kriya yoga is designed for individuals who find it difficult to sit still and stay focused for a long time. But - everyone should, whether you are tamasic, rajasic or sattvic, practice Hatha yoga as a preparation. A tamasic person needs Hatha yoga to awaken the mind and body. A person who is rajasic needs Hatha yoga to balance the vital and mental energies in the body and mind. A sattvic person needs Hatha yoga to make it easier to awaken Kundalini. In other words, Hatha yoga is for everyone and a preparation for Kriya yoga. If you have practiced asanas, pranayamas, mudras and bandhas regularly for two years, you are usually ready for Kriya yoga.

There are many Kriyas but twenty of these are the most important and powerful. These twenty are divided into two groups. The first nine are done with open eyes and the remaining eleven are done with closed eyes.

In the first group of exercises, it is important that you really do not close your eyes even if you feel very relaxed and have an easy time turning your mind inward. You can blink, rest, take a break but do not close your eyes.

The first Kriyan is called Vipareeta Karani mudra. It is a method of creating a reverse process in the body. In Hatha Yoga Pradipika and the old tantric texts you can read about this process:

This nectar originates from the moon. As the sun consumes this nectar, the yogi ages. His body collapses and dies. Through regular practice, the yogi should try to reverse this process. The nectar flowing from the moon (Bindu) towards the sun (Manipura) should be returned to the higher centers. When the flow of amrit or nectar can be reversed, it will not be consumed by the sun. It will instead be assimilated by the body."

When the body has been cleansed with Hatha yoga, pranayamas and a pure diet the nectar of the body is assimilated and one experiences a higher mental state. The mind is still and you see and hear everything much clearer.

It is said that one can influence and control the structure and energy of the body and thus evoke peace, dharana, dhyana or samadhi. The various exercises in Kriya yoga such as Vipareeta Karani mudra, Amrit Pan, Khechari mudra, Moola bandha, Maha mudra, and Maha Bheda mudra, regulate the nervous system. The prana in the body is harmonized and balanced. You achieve a state of peace and tranquility without having to fight against the mind. All this by creating a flow of unused and natural chemicals in the body. Amrit is one of them and through Khechari mudra you can make it flow.

Khechari mudra is a simple but very important technique used in most kriyas. By turning the tongue upwards in the palate towards the nasal passage, specific glands and bandages are stimulated, resulting in the amrite starting to flow. One experiences shoonyata, a state of nothingness, being and awareness of everything. Body temperature drops and alpha waves begin to prevail. The mind is completely still.

When you have practiced yoga for a while and have reached the point where you have achieved concentration and a complete inner stillness in body, mind and soul but still feel that there is more to discover, you are ready for Kriya yoga. A calm mind, relaxed body and the right understanding are the results of a spiritual life, however, it is not the ultimate goal. The deeper meaning of yoga is to change the character of the experience, the pattern of the mind and its perception. Man's purpose in practicing yoga has been to expand the mind and release energy. It is tantra and the ultimate goal of Kriya yoga.

"That is the sign of wisdom: freedom from desire. Only fools desire. Wise people live and live joyously, but without desire. Either you can desire or you can live, you can not do both. If you desire, you postpone living; if you live, who bothers about desiring? Today is enough unto itself."

THE CHAKRA SYSTEM

THE CHAKRA SYSTEM
In tantra and yoga, the lotus flower is used as a symbol for chakras. Man's spiritual development consists of three important phases: ignorance, striving, or, longing and enlightenment. In the same way, the lotus flower grows through three phases: clay, water and air. It grows in mud (ignorance), grows up through the water to the surface (striving and longing), and finally it comes up from the water and reaches the air and sunlight (enlightenment).

Each chakra is described as a lotus flower with a specific color and a number of petals. Each chakra consists of six different aspects:

1. Colour
2. Number of petals
3. Yantra (geometric shape)
4. Beeja mantra (sound / vibration)
5. Animal symbol (represents previous stages of evolution)
6. Higher / eternal being (represents the higher consciousness).

OUR CHAKRA

We have lots of chakras in our body but the most important ones are along our spine. There are also hidden so-called "Secret chakras".
The eight most important chakras in our body are:

MOOLADHARA CHAKRA

The root chakra is located at the base of the spine and is the chakra that vibrates with the lowest frequency, ie. the slowest of our seven chakras. Due to its frequency, its color is dark red and it has four petals. The element associated with this chakra is earth and stands for the most physical and down-to-earth with us.

SWADHISTHANA CHAKRA

The Swadhisthana chakra is located about two centimeters above the tailbone and is the center of our sexuality and reproductive ability. It has six petals, the color orange and its element is water.

MANIPURA CHAKRA

The Manipura chakra is located at the spine at the level of the solar plexus. It has ten petals and the color is yellow. The element fire controls Manipura and it is associated with will, worldly pursuit, ambition and career.

ANAHATA CHAKRA

The Anahatha chakra is located in the spine behind the heart. It has twelve petals and the color is blue or green depending on the tradition you are studying. The element air dominates the chakra and controls our emotions and the relationship with other people. The Anahata chakra is also a symbol of love.

VISHUDDHI CHAKRA

Vishuddhi chakra is located in the neck and has sixteen petals. The color is violet and the element is space (ether). It controls our communication with the environment on different levels.

AJNA CHAKRA

The Ajna chakra is located in the middle of the head at the pineal gland and its contact area is the eyebrow center. It controls our paranormal abilities and Siddhis. Also called guru chakra or third eye. It is white in color and has two petals. It is associated with the mind, reason, intelligence and intuition.

BINDU VISARGA

According to tantra, Bindu visarga is a point located on the back of the head, where the Brahmins usually have their tuft of hair. It represents the crescent with a white drop, which stands for the manifestation of creation, such as consciousness.

SAHASRARA CHAKRA

The chakra is located just above the head and is purple / red in color. It has a thousand petals and represents pure consciousness. When Kundalini shakti reaches Sahasrara chakra we become enlightened and according to yoga we enter nirvikalpa samadhi.

KSHETRAM

The exercises in Kundalini yoga usually focus on the trigger point of the chakra, which has its place at the spine. It can be difficult to experience in the beginning and many find it easier to focus on the point of contact on the front of the body called the chakra Kshetram. When we focus on a Kshetram, a sensation is created which then passes via the nerve pathways to the chakra and from there up to the brain. Mooladhara has no contact point, or, Kshetram.

GRANTHIS

We have three granthis (mental knots) in our physical body that are obstacles to Kundalini. These are called Brahma, Vishnu and Rudra. They describe the strength of the Maya, the ignorance and the attraction to material things. Level of consciousness. As an aspirant, one must overcome these obstacles in order for Kundalini to flow unhindered.

Brahma granthi has its place in the Mooladhara chakra and is associated with desire for material things, physical satisfaction and selfishness. It is also responsible for tamas - negativity, lethargy and ignorance.

Vishnu granthi has its place at the Anahata chakra and is associated with emotional desires, depending on people and inner mental visions. It is linked to rajas and has tendencies towards passion, ambition and determination.

Rudra granthi rules over the Ajna chakra. It is associated with the desire for Siddhis, mental phenomena and the image of ourselves as individuals.

THE EVOLUTION THROUGH THE CHAKRANA

Human evolution as individuals and as a race is a journey through our chakras. Mooladhara is the base and Sahasrara is the very goal or end of evolution.

In animals, Mooladhara is the highest chakra. It is their Sahasrara. Until Mooladhara, evolution takes place by itself, it is under the control of nature. When Kundalini reaches Mooladhara, evolution no longer happens automatically. Man is no longer subordinate to the laws of nature. Man is aware of time and space. Man has an ego, he can think, is aware that he is thinking and he knows that he is aware that he is thinking. Without the ego, there is no double consciousness. Animals do not have a double consciousness. Man thus has a higher consciousness and must therefore also work to develop it. Therefore, it is said that Kundalini lies dormant in Mooladhara until it is awakened for further development.

Awakening Kundalini is a process. It may wake up to return to Mooladhara several times. When it finally reaches the Manipura chakra in a steady state, it will not turn again. What can happen is that it can get stuck in a chakra if there are blockages or if the sushumna is not open. Kundalini can remain in a chakra for several years or even a lifetime.

Before starting to practice Kundalini yoga, it is important to find out in which chakra Kundalini is located. The easiest way to do this is to focus on each chakra individually for fifteen minutes over a fifteen day period. You will notice which chakra is easiest to experience and stay focused on. Here is Kundalini shakti.

Awakening our chakras plays an important role in human evolution. It has nothing to do with mystery or anything occult. When the chakras are awakened, our consciousness and our mind change. This affects our daily lives as our mind is what controls how we act in different situations, relationships and emotions.

Today, many children are born with open chakras and Kundalini. When these children grow up, they behave differently. Our modern society often sees these differences as something abnormal and the result is often mental health care or similar. Going through conflicts

The Chakranas
Colour, Number of Petals, Yantra
Action. Element & Bija mantra

Sahasrara chakra – I understand
dark red, 1000 petals. Aum, Shiva

Ajna chakra	Third Eye
White, 2 Petals	I see
Pyramid	Moon Aum
Vishuddhi chakra	I talk
Purple 16 petals	Space Element
Cirkel with Space	Bija mantra Ham
Anahatha chakra	I love
Blue, 12 petals	Air element
Blue davidsstar	Bija mantra Yam
Manipura chakra	I do
Yellow, 10 petals	Fire element
Red triangel	Bija mantra Ram
Swadhisthana ch.	I feel
Orange, 6 petals	Water element
Half moon	Bija mantra Vam

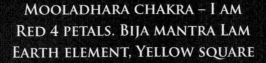

Mooladhara chakra – I am
Red 4 petals. Bija mantra Lam
Earth element, Yellow square

within family and work is a common phenomenon, but when the mind and consciousness begin to expand, one becomes extremely sensitive to everything that happens in the mind, family, colleagues and society. You can not overlook something that happens in life. It is not seen as normal by most people but it is a natural consequence of the chakra being awakened. Consciousness becomes very receptive when the frequency of the mind changes.

Love, devotion, charity, etc. are all expressions of a mind affected by the chakra in balance. This is the reason why so much emphasis is placed on awakening the Anahata chakra, or, the heart chakra. All chakras are of course important to open up and all have different qualities, but you can see that in most ancient scriptures put extra emphasis on awakening the Anahata, Ajna and Mooladhara chakra. When Anahata is awakened, we get a deeper relationship with our family and all individuals.

When the chakras are opened, the mind changes automatically. Values change and love and relationships change character. Disappointments and feelings of frustration are balanced, which leads to a better attitude towards ourselves and life.

PREPARATIONS FOR KRIYA YOGA
Kriya yoga is considered by many to be the most effective method of developing human consciousness. These exercises are said to be those that Shiva gave to his wife, Parvati. Kriyas are relatively simple and not too powerful for the average person to perform.

Before you start practicing Kriya yoga, it is important that you can feel the chakras in the body, both mentally and physically, and to be able to locate its Kshetram. One should also know two mental passages in the body "arohan" and "awarohan".

In order to develop in Kundalini yoga and in preparation for Kriya yoga, it is important to be well acquainted with the following techniques:

Vipareeta karani asana
Ujjayi pranayama
Siddhasana / Siddha yoni asana
Unmani mudra
Khechari mudra

Ajapa Japa
Utthanpadasana
Shambhavi mudra
Moola bandha
Nasikagra drishti
Uddiyana bandha
Jalandhara bandha
Bhadrasana
Padmasana
Shanmuki mudra
Varjoli / Sahajoli mudra

IDA AND PINGALA
Yogis have described that man has three main flows of energy in the body. Ida, pingala and sushumna nadi. These can be roughly translated as mind, body and spirit. Sushumna is the result of a balanced and harmonious flow between ida and pingala.

Nadis are flows of energy that move throughout our body. All the thousands of nadis that flow in the body are connected to the ida and pingala nadi that move along the spine. Every cell in our body, every organ, brain and mind are linked on a mental and physical level, which allows us to speak, think and act in a balanced and correct way. Ida and pingala nadi are the ones who control the balance between them. By affecting a part of the system, the whole system is affected. This is how asanas, pranayamas, meditation and the whole yogic system work. Yoga thus affects the entire system of nadis in our body.

Yogis and scientists have come to the same result, albeit with different ways of describing it. Man has two main modes through which he functions. The pattern of the brain is based on ida and pingala nadi, consciousness or knowledge, action or physical energy. We can see ida and pingala nadis functions in the three main parts of the nervous system.

Sensory-motor nervous system where all electrical activity in the body moves within two paths through the body. Into the brain (afferent), ida and out through the brain (efferent), pingala. Autonomic nervous system which is divided into the outward, stress management, energy utilization, pingala dominant, sympathetic nervous system and inward, relaxed, energy saving, ida dominant parasympathetic nervous system.

Central nervous system which consists of the brain and spine and which controls the two preceding parts of the nervous system.

What the yogic techniques are based on is the knowledge of our nadis and chakras. The physical experience of these that you can also experience on a physical level through the different parts of the nervous system. The influence of the nervous system on our physical body describes the importance of balancing and harmonizing the flow between ida, pingala and sushumna nadi.

THE IMPORTANCE OF PREPARATION, EXERCISE AND NOT TAKING WATER OVER YOUR HEAD

As a beginner in yoga and full of desire and inspiration, it is easy to get water over your head. Yoga is a process in which the body and mind are prepared for more advanced techniques. It's like running. If you have run several marathons, you may need to run longer stretches to feel that the training gives something. This does not mean that you as a new runner do not get the benefits out of running three kilometers. This is exactly how yoga works.

When you have practiced Hatha yoga for a few years and feel comfortable in the positions with all the locks and postures and master the breathing exercises, you can move on with the most advanced tantric techniques. Then they will not feel too complicated and you will have a consciousness that allows you to enjoy the effects of your practice without it becoming too much. If something feels too complicated or difficult, go back one step instead. Everything comes to you when you are ready. Hurry slowly.

"You experience all the power in the cosmos and on earth, in yourself and around. Everything you want is possible because all power is yours!"

CHAKRANA INDEX

AJNA CHAKRA

AJNA CHAKRA

ALSO CALLED THIRD EYE

TANMATRA (sensory experience): Sense.

JNANENDRIYA (sense organ): Sense.

KARMENDRIYA (body of action): Sense.

TATTWA (element): Sense.

BEJA MANTRA: Om.

TATTWA SYMBOL: Picture of the mantra Om.

YOGA TYPE: Jnana, Raja and Mantra yoga (Sattvic).

LOTUS (PADMA): White, silver or smoky with two petals.

AJNA CHAKRA (third eye) is associated with the mind, reason, intelligence and intuition. It is also the center through which two people through the mind - on a deeper level, are in contact with each other. For example, the contact between guru (teacher / master) and student / disciple.

Direct concentration on the Ajna chakra is very difficult and therefore one focuses on tantra and yoga in the middle of the eyebrow center (which is in fact the Kshetram of the Ajna chakra). This point is called bhrumadhya (bhru- refers to eyebrows and -madhya refers to the center), and lies between the eyebrows at the place where Indian ladies put a red dot and Pandits and Brahmins put a mark. This eyebrow center can be touched by various techniques.

Ajna and Mooladhara chakras are closely related, and awakening in one of these helps to awaken the others. Ideally, Ajna should be awakened to some extent before Mooladhara in order to prepare the mind for all the hidden memories and impressions that come to the surface as we practice chakra awakening. But the awakening in Mooladhara will also help to further awaken Ajna. In fact, the best way to bring about the awakening of Ajna is Moola bandha and Ashwini mudra, which are specific to Mooladhara.

It should also be mentioned that the Ajna chakra and the pineal gland are one and the same. Just like the pituitary gland is the physical aspect of Sahasrara. The pituitary gland and the pineal gland are intimately connected to each other, as are the Ajna and Sahasrara. We can say that Ajna is the gateway to the Sahasrara chakra. If Ajna is awakened and works, then all experiences in Sahasrara happen as well.

The pineal gland acts as a lock for the pituitary gland. As long as the pineal gland is healthy, the pituitary gland works on a deeper, spiritual level. But for most of us, the pineal gland stops developing when we turn eight, nine or ten years old. This is when the pituitary gland begins to function and secrete various hormones that stimulate our sexual consciousness, our sensuality and worldly person. At this time, we started to lose touch with our spiritual heritage. However, through various yogic techniques, such as Trataka and Shambhavi mudra, it is possible to restore or maintain the health of the pineal gland. The pineal gland and Ajna chakra have a special significance in esoteric yoga and in tantra. It is the place where Siddhis (magical) abilities are manifested.

The "third eye" is a mysterious and esoteric concept that can refer to Ajna chakra in various spiritual traditions from East and West. It is also said to be a door that leads into inner worlds and stages of higher consciousness. In tantra and yoga, the "third eye" can symbolize enlightenment or the development of mental images with deeply spiritual or psychological meanings. The "third eye" is often associated with Siddhis such as revelations, clairvoyance (which also includes the ability to observe chakras and auras), divination, and out-of-body experiences. A person who is considered to have developed an ability to use his "third eye" is called a Siddha in yoga, and is referred to as a person who has developed Siddhis.

"The pineal gland and the DMT molecule - the third eye ... there may be a way for the brain to actually take us to a higher plane of existence, where we can understand the world and our relationships to things and people on a deeper level and where we can ultimately create a deeper meaning for ourselves and our world. There is a spiritual part of the brain - it is a part that we can all have access to and is something that we all can accomplish."

(Andrew Newberg - brain researcher)

MOOLADHARA CHAKRA

MOOLADHARA CHAKRA

TANMATRA (sensory experience): Smell.

JNANENDRIYA (sense organ): Nose.

KARMENDRIYA (organ of action): Anus.

TATTWA (element): Prithvi (earth).

BIJA MANTRA: Lam.

TATTWA SYMBOL: Yellow square.

ANIMALS: Elephant.

YOGA TYPE: Tantra and Hatha yoga (counteracts tamas / inertia).

LOTUS (PADMA): Red lotus with four petals.

MOOLADHARA CHAKRA
Moola means root. A triangular space in the middle of the body at a point between the genitals and anus for men and at the cervix for women. Mooladhara is associated with personal security in both thought and action. At this

level, the individual focuses mainly on obtaining food and shelter and to secure his reproduction. She surrounds herself with material things, money, family and friends in order to create personal security.

In the middle of Mooladhara, one usually imagines a black swayambhu linga (a symbol of male power, Shiva). Around this, the serpent Kundalini (Shakti, the mother of all prana in the human body) winds three and a half turns - dozing in anticipation of its awakening, as it ascends through sushumna nadi to unite with Shiva in Sahasrara padma in the moment of enlightenment. This can only happen when the individual's spiritual development has reached the necessary maturity.

MOOLADHARA'S IMPACT ON OUR DIFFERENT BODIES

IN ANNAMAYA KOSHA (physical body).
Reproductive organs, perineum, uterine tube.

IN PRANAMAYA KOSHA (energy body).
Apana vayu.

IN MANOMAYA KOSHA (body of thought).
Security, ownership, safety, survival.

MOOLADHARA IN DIFFERENT STAGES OF GUNAS

Creation and its energy consist of three gunas, fundamental properties or tendencies: Sattva, rajas and tamas. These three gunas act and react incessantly with each other. The world of phenomena is composed of different combinations of these three gunas. Tamas stands for inertia, rajas for movement and sattva for balance. When Mooladhara is in balance and sattvic, we are safe and secure in ourselves and in the world. When Mooladhara is out of balance and is tamasic, we experience boundless fear. We are in a deep psychosis. As the balance becomes more rajasic, our condition changes as shown below. By identifying one's state with the right degree of imbalance / balance in the various chakras, the yogi believes that he can alleviate and dissolve negative states.

TAMAS: Horror.

TAMAS / RAJAS: Anxiety, worries.

RAJAS / TAMAS: Greed, self-confidence.

RAJAS: Collector.

RAJAS / SATTVA: Generosity.

SATTVA / RAJAS: Property for good cause.

SATTVA: Safe in the physical world.

ENLIGHTENED: Unity with the absolute

SWADHISTHANA

SWADHISTHANA CHAKRA

TANMATRA (sensory experience): Taste.

JNANENDRIYA (sense organ): Tongue.

KARMENDRIYA (organ of action): Genitals.

TATTWA (element): Apas (water).

BIJA MANTRA: Vam.

TATTWA SYMBOL: White crescent.

ANIMALS: Crocodile.

YOGA TYPE: Tantra and Hatha yoga (counteracts tamas / inertia).

LOTUS (PADMA): Orange lotus with six petals.

SWADHISTHANA CHAKRA (pleasure, lust)
The chakra sits at the base of the spine just inside the lower tailbone and at the height of the genitals. Chakra is associated with senso-

ry experiences. One strives to achieve sensory enjoyment through e.g. food, drinks, sex, etc. You value everything in terms of the enjoyment you can thereby achieve. The difference from the Mooladhara chakra is that here we strive for the pleasure of the mind itself, rather than for satisfying the basic needs.

It is said that most people in the world primarily act and are motivated at this level. Swadhisthana chakra is also usually associated with the unconscious. It is said that coexistence - traces or patterns created in the unconscious of the experiences we make and the actions we perform, have their place in this chakra. Samskaras eventually form the basis of the individual's karma. Most of these cohabitants are displaced from consciousness or can be even repressed. Therefore, the Swadhisthana chakra is often associated with desires, urges, and fears over which we have no control.

THE IMPACT OF SWADHISTANS IN OUR DIFFERENT BODIES

ANNAMAYA KOSHA (physical body): Genitals, urination.

PRANAMAYA KOSHA (energy body): Apana vayu.

MANOMAYA KOSHA (body of thought): Satisfaction, pleasure, sex (from pleasure to addiction).

SWADHISTHANA IN DIFFERENT STAGES OF GUNAS

TAMAS: Depression.

TAMAS / RAJAS: Bitterness, feeling of being rejected.

RAJAS / TAMAS: Desire, sexual exploitation.

RAJAS: Seeking pleasure, sexual conquests.

RAJAS / SATTVA: Humor, caring sexuality with love.

SATTVA / RAJAS: Happily satisfied.

SATTVA: Bubbly happy.

ENLIGHTENED: Ananda, happiness "bliss".

MANIPURA CHAKRA

MANIPURA CHAKRA

TANMATRA (sensory experience): Vision.

JNANENDRIYA (sensory organs): Eyes.

KARMENDRIYA (organ of action): Feet.

TATTWA (element): Agni (fire).

BIJA MANTRA: Ram.

TATTWA SYMBOL: Red inverted triangle.

ANIMALS: Aries.

YOGA TYPE: Karma yoga (counteracts rajas / mobility).

LOTUS (PADMA): Yellow lotus with ten petals.

MANIPURA (seat of the jewel)
The chakra is located in the spine at the level of the navel. It is associated with will, worldly pursuit, ambition and career. From the energy of manipulation, man grows as a social and self-conscious being. She cultivates material

desires, such as owning and mastering, power, prestige and usefulness. But also selflessness, social balance and prosperity.

Manipura's energy is outward and active, a vital energy that provides the power to act and the power to change oneself and one's surroundings. Sometimes this happens with a selfish attitude where other people are seen as a means to achieve their own ambition, but here also the first expressions of a growing self-awareness begin to take shape in man. The ego is still dominant but the first traces of a genuine, spiritual pursuit are manifested at this level. One begins to seriously question one's existence and one's motives.

THE IMPACT OF MANIPURAS IN OUR DIFFERENT BODIES

ANNAMAYA KOSHA (physical body): Solar Plexus, digestion.

PRANAMAYA KOSHA (energy body): Samana vayu.

MANOMAYA KOSHA (body of thought): Power, action, self-confidence and striving.

MANIPURA IN DIFFERENT STAGES OF GUNAS

TAMAS: Inability to act.

TAMAS / RAJAS: Guilt over non-actions, low self-esteem.

RAJAS / TAMAS: Frustration over one's own inability.

RAJAS: Active, brave.

RAJAS / SATTVA: Anxious, ready to act.

SATTVA / RAJAS: Karma yoga at an intermediate level.

SATTVA: Things happen as if by miracle.

ENLIGHTENED: Omnipotent.

"And when love goes deeper,
fear disappears.

love is the light, fear is darkness."

ANAHATA CHAKRA

ANAHATA CHAKRA

TANMATRA (sensory experience): Feeling.

JNANENDRIYA (sense organ): Skin.

KARMENDRIYA (body of action): Hands.

TATTWA (element): Vayu (air).

BIJA MANTRA: Yam.

TATTWA SYMBOL: Blue hexagram.

ANIMALS: Black antelope.

YOGA TYPE: Bhakti and Karma yoga (counteracts rajas / mobility).

LOTUS (PADMA): Blue or green lotus with twelve petals.

ANAHATA (unspoken "sound", the origin of all mantras). Anahatha sits in the spine at the height of the heart. Its energy is associated with love, hate, joy and sorrow as well as with the beauty experience. Chakra is strongly associated with our relationships with others around us.

At this level, the individual often begins to love everything and everyone unconditionally. You learn to ignore the faults and shortcomings of others and take them for what they are. Anahata also stands for aesthetic discernment and artistic creation. The energy is expressed here in the form of creativity regardless of which area you are active in. At this level, man leaves the material world to cultivate higher values.

THE INFLUENCE OF ANAHATAS IN OUR DIFFERENT BODIES

ANNAMAYA KOSHA (physical body): Heart, lungs.

PRANAMAYA KOSHA (energy body): Vyana vayu.

MANOMAYA KOSHA (body of thought): Love, compassion, acceptance and tolerance.

ANAHATHA IN DIFFERENT STAGES OF GUNAS

TAMAS: Apathy.

TAMAS / RAJAS: Fraud, treason.

RAJAS / TAMAS: Avoid intimacy.

RAJAS: Love under certain conditions.

RAJAS / SATTVA: Care about others.

SATTVA / RAJAS: Love and compassion.

SATTVA: Is love.

ENLIGHTENED: Cosmic love.

VISHUDDHI CHAKRA

VISHUDDHI CHAKRA

TANMATRA (sensory experience): Sound.

JNANENDRIYA (sensory organs): Ears.

KARMENDRIYA (body of action): Body of speech.

TATTWA (element): Akasha (space).

BIJA MANTRA: Ham.

TATTWA SYMBOL: White and black circle.

ANIMALS: White elephant.

YOGA TYPE: Jnana, Raja and Mantra yoga (sattvic)

LOTUS (PADMA): Violet lotus with sixteen petals.

VISHUDDHI (purity).
The chakra sits in the neck behind the larynx and is associated with an attitude of independence (vairagya), where both pleasant and

unpleasant aspects of human life are seen and accepted as rewarding experiences. The world appears as a place full of harmony and perfection. Everything you experience, good or bad, is seen as part of a whole that helps to remove personal problems, locks and limitations and raise the level of consciousness. This attitude leads to discernment (viveka).

Vishuddhi is also associated with expression, communication in general and the spoken word in particular.

THE IMPACT OF VISHUDDIS IN OUR DIFFERENT BODIES

ANNAMAYA KOSHA (physical body): The thyroid gland, parathyroid gland, trachea and esophagus.

PRANAMAYA KOSHA (energy body): Udana vayu.

MANOMAYA KOSHA (body of thought): Communication.

VISHUDDHI IN DIFFERENT STAGES OF GUNAS

TAMAS: Isolated.

TAMAS / RAJAS: Limited contact / communication.

RAJAS / TAMAS: Complaining / whining.

RAJAS: Pretty good communicator.

RAJAS / SATTVA: Eloquent.

SATTVA / RAJAS: Persuader, non-violent communication.

SATTVA: True communication.

ENLIGHTENED: Cosmic communication.

BINDU VISARGA

Bindu visarga is located on top of the back of the head. Many claim that one can not find Bindu in the physical body but that it can only be experienced via nada, ie. via its vibration or sound. It is not really a chakra in the ordinary sense.

Through techniques like Moorcha pranayama and Vajroli / Sahajoli mudra we can develop the experience of nada and through techniques like Bhramari pranayama and Shanmukhi mudra we can follow nada to its source - Bindu.

There is a close relationship between the Swadhisthana chakra and the Bindu. This is because Bindu is the point where the vibration and sound of the individual creation is first manifested, and Swadhisthana is the center of creation in the form of sexual reproduction. Through Swadhisthana, our physical desire for union with the cosmic consciousness is expressed. Sperm and menstruation are physical expressions of the drops of amrit - the nectar drops of creation or secretions that drip from the Bindu and are burned in the Manipura chakra via the Vishuddhi chakra. The drops that control the creation process and the body's aging.

It is commonly believed that there is no Kshetram - contact point for Bindu visarga.

SAHASRARA CHAKRA

The chakra is located just above the head and is purple / red in color. It has a thousand petals and represents pure consciousness. When Kundalini shakti reaches Sahasrara chakra we become enlightened and according to yoga we enter Nirvikalpa samadhi.

The function of the Sahasrara is to provide us with other levels of consciousness, which may make us realize that "we are one" and that "everything is one". It is through the crown chakra that we experience union with God and with the supernatural. The Crown Chakra is what is called "pure consciousness".

When one reaches the higher level of consciousness in this chakra, all thinking is released. Here lay the answers to all our questions, the absolute truth that we all dream of getting answers to, and where we find total freedom - We become enlightened.

Printed in Great Britain
by Amazon